NEW COURAGE FOR DAILY LIVING

DEVOTIONS FOR ADULTS

BY MARTIN H. FRANZMANN

CONCORDIA PUBLISHING HOUSE

SAINT LOUIS

CONCORDIA PUBLISHING HOUSE, ST. LOUIS, MISSOURI

CONCORDIA PUBLISHING HOUSE LTD., LONDON, W.C.1.

COPYRIGHT 1963 BY CONCORDIA PUBLISHING HOUSE

Library of Congress Catalog Card No. 63-19962

MANUFACTURED IN THE UNITED STATES OF AMERICA

PREFACE

Each of us no doubt has his favorite book or books in the New Testament, books that speak with especial directness and warmth to his heart. I confess that Paul's Letter to the Colossians was not one of mine. I appreciated it and valued it as the very word of God to me, of course; I could not do otherwise as a baptized man. But I turned instinctively to other books in the New Testament for answers to my questions and my needs, to Paul's Letter to the Romans, to the Letter of James, to the Gospel According to Matthew. God has ways of making us enlarge our horizons; it was not until I was asked to write a series of devotions on the Letter to the Colossians that I became fully alive to the riches of the letter, riches of insight and knowledge, riches of inspiration and encouragement, riches of help and strength. If this little book helps others to a similar discovery, I shall feel that a gracious Lord has rewarded me richly. I hope, too, that others will be encouraged to look beyond their favorite books and go farther afield in God's green pastures than heretofore. I can assure them that they will be the better and the braver for it.

MARTIN H. FRANZMANN

A Voice in Our Darkness

Paul, an apostle of Jesus Christ by the will of God. Col. 1:1

A child wakes up in the night afraid and cries out. The only answer that will quiet his fear is his mother's steady voice: "I'm here." The close presence, the near sound, the assured voice of the beloved person — these are the only cure for fear.

We are all of us children in the dark; we are none of us grown so big that we have outgrown our fear of the dark. We live fear-filled lives in a fear-filled world. We know ourselves better, perhaps, than men have ever known themselves before; psychology has contributed to that. And we grow steadily more fearful of ourselves and of one another. We have mastered the world about us as men have never mastered it before; but this mastered world grows more mysterious by the hour, and our fear of it grows with our knowledge of it. Our generation cries:

> . . . What am I?
> An infant crying in the night,
> An infant crying for the light,
> And with no language but a cry.

Into this darkness comes the voice of God and speaks to us: "I am here." It *is* the voice of God; Paul speaks to us as an apostle "by the will of God." God took Paul against Paul's willing and contrary to Paul's running, turned him completely round, and gave him His very Word to speak. It is the voice of God that we are privileged to hear when we open our Bibles and turn to the Letter of Paul to the Colossians. For Paul is an apostle, a messenger, of Jesus Christ; and Jesus has said of His apostles: "He who receives you receives Me, and he who receives Me receives Him who sent Me." (Matthew 10:40)

The voice of God reaches us in the dark. It really reaches us; it comes all the way to us in our darkness as a human voice calling in human fashion into our human life. Paul is the messenger and the bringer of Jesus Christ: Jesus Christ speaks in him. The Son of God, who humbled Himself and came and dwelt in our darkness, speaks in Paul. One who has felt our fears speaks in him; this is the voice of the One who has cried out in our darkness, "My God, My God, why hast Thou forsaken Me?" Here is the voice of One who has tasted our human terror to the full that we might be forever freed from fear. Here is the voice of One who by His death in darkness for us has become the Light that shines in the darkness, a Light which the darkness shall never overcome.

His messenger Paul, through whom Christ speaks to us, is no gold-plated saint, bloodless and fearless; he does not speak to us from a pedestal. He is a man who has known fear. He is a man who has collapsed in a terror like ours and has then heard the voice of Christ, "Rise and stand upon your feet." He never became so fearless a man that we fearful men cannot claim him as kin; when there was "fighting without," he felt "fear within" (2 Corinthians 7:5). But he was a man who again and again found the strength to fight down his fear; he found this strength in the God who comforts the downcast, in Christ, who strengthened him. He it is who speaks here as a messenger of Jesus Christ; he speaks the Word of God to us. He calls us his brothers, and he speaks a language which we can understand. In his word we have the close presence, the near sound, the assured voice of the Beloved Person, the voice of God, the God who loves us with an everlasting love and tells us, "I am here."

PRAYER. O God, who hast spoken to us in Thy beloved Son and hast told us, "Fear no more!" give us Thy Spirit that we hear Thy voice in the words of the apostle of Jesus Christ and, hearing, fear the darkness no more. Amen.

The Test of Courage

We always thank God, the Father of our Lord Jesus Christ, when we pray for you. Col. 1:3

God's voice reaches us in our darkness and gives us courage. Courage is tested, always. If there were nothing in this life to test our courage, we should not have the word courage in our vocabulary at all. This new Christian courage of ours will be tested too. We usually think of high heroic moments when we think of tests of courage; we think of being thrown to the lions or being burned at the stake. But it is not given to many of us to show our courage in this bold, dramatic way. For most of us life brings a series of little, undramatic tests. These tests come again and again, and it is this endless repetition that makes this kind of testing difficult and hard to bear. One test which we must meet repeatedly is this: Have we the courage to give thanks? That is, have we been really set free from our little fears and our anxieties? Are we free to see and to set a proper value on the gifts of God?

We do not meet this test by thinking about it; we pass this test by doing. Begin now. Perhaps you are reading this at breakfast. Begin by going through the exercise of counting your blessings: the good night's sleep, the sunlight streaming through the window (or the good rain watering the earth for the just and the unjust), the food so good and so plentiful — if you are dieting, thank God for that; He has given you so much that you are forced to select, and He has given you the sense to be selective.

Or perhaps you are reading this in the evening; then thank God for the blessings of a good day's work, for the opportunities to witness which He has given you this day, for bringing you safely home through the evening traffic. Do not stop there; King Solomon in all his glory did not have the luxuries that you enjoy: light at the flick of a switch, warm water at the turn of a tap, the world's news spoken into your ear while you sit at ease in your living room. Take a good look at what the Father of our Lord Jesus Christ has given you. If you cannot thank Him for these things, you have not heard His voice to any purpose.

But this test of courage is only a preliminary; the real test is still coming. Can you give thanks, as Paul does, for others? When did you last give thanks for your spouse, your children, your relatives, your neighbors? And have you ever given thanks for the people whom you have never seen and may not ever see? Have you grown free and bold enough to thank the Father for those unknown millions who unite with you whenever you pray, "Our Father"? Have you thanked Him for the witness of those thousands who strengthen us by suffering for the faith which they hold with us?

Or to come close to home again, how many of us thank God for the preacher and pastor whom He has set before us to speak His Word to us? Is that why "we get so little out of the sermon"? Is it because our thanklessness has made an audience of us, cool, self-satisfied, and critical, insulated against the sermon by our ingratitude?

Our Lord was a Man of thankfulness: He thanked His Father for the gifts He received from the Father's hand. He never broke bread without giving thanks for it. The disciples at Emmaus recognized Him when they saw Him giving thanks for bread as He had always done at every meal with them.

PRAYER. O God, the Father of our Lord Jesus Christ, give us ears to hear Thy voice; set us free from fear and from ourselves, free to behold the wonders of Thy grace and to give Thee thanks. **Amen.**

Courage to Pray

And so . . . we have not ceased to pray for you, asking that you may be filled with the knowledge of His will in all spiritual wisdom and understanding, to lead a life worthy of the Lord, fully pleasing to Him, bearing fruit in every good work and increasing in the knowledge of God. Col. 1:9, 10

"And so" — Paul turns from thanking to asking. There is nothing like thanksgiving to make a man bold in prayer. Our grateful saying of "Our Father" turns our eyes to the Father of our Lord Jesus Christ, who gave His Son for us and makes us bold and free to ask Him for all things; the petitions which span all the blessings of the world to come and the asking for our daily bread follow almost as a matter of course. The thankful heart is bold in prayer.

The thankful heart is also a large heart. The God who set us free from sin has set us free for Himself and therefore free for one another. When He makes us His sons, He endows us with His will of love; we draw our life from Him and live our life in harmony with His will. The old classic prayer of selfishness —

> Bless me and my wife,
> Son John and his wife,
> Us four,
> And no more —

that prayer has become impossible for us. Our prayers embrace the whole family of God — and the whole world that He sent His Son to save.

The grateful heart is a wise heart; it is open to God and knows and has God's gifts. The thankful man can therefore pray for the best gift. What better gift is there than to know God's will, to have that wisdom which God's Spirit creates in us, that understanding which the Spirit alone can give us? To have that wisdom and understanding is to see God steadily and see Him whole. To know His will is to know Him personally and powerfully; it means being caught up in His motion as He moves through history in might and mercy to bring home His sons to the Father's house for life with Himself. To be caught up thus means a fruitful life, a life filled with good works, a life upon which the Father can smile His pleasure. Living this life, we walk through the world like children happy in the sunshine of their parents' love. We cannot go back to our childhood; but we can find again the serenity and security of our childhood, and we can pray this blessing down on others.

Surely this is wisdom, to know this best gift and to pray for it; for this gift is never used up or worn out. Rather it is continually renewing itself and is a perpetual glad surprise. The more a man draws on the knowledge of God for his living, and the more he uses the knowledge given him, the deeper his knowledge of God becomes. Day by day and year by year the obedient child grows in the knowledge of his father's love for him. And God, who delights to give, rewards our every good work (forgiving all that is amiss in it) by binding us more closely to Himself.

PRAYER. Give me a heart, O God, to thank Thee for Thy love; make me so large and free and wise in heart that I can seek in prayer Thy best gift for my brethren everywhere; through Jesus Christ, Thy Son, our Lord. Amen.

The Great Good Place

He has delivered us from the dominion of darkness and trans-ferred us to the kingdom of His beloved Son, in whom we have redemption, the forgiveness of sins. Col. 1:13, 14

That very secular writer, Henry James, in a story called *The Great Good Place,* once sketched a heaven of his heart's desire. It is a charming sketch, this picture of a quiet refuge from the pressures of life, with its general air of lightness, spaciousness, and unclutteredness, where men's wants are quietly and perfectly taken care of and they can luxuriate in the "uncontested possession of the long, sweet, stupid day." It is a shining, placid, and sophisticated paradise.

It is easy to criticize James's paradise. It is too ex-clusive — for intellectuals only, no place for the agony of downtrodden stupid people. And release from pressure is, after all, not paradise, however much we may think so when we are under heavy pressure. In the last analysis there is something chilly and empty about James's heaven; no one could endure it for long, as James himself well knew; he designed his paradise as an interlude, not as an eternity. But the chief criticism is of course the obvious one: James's paradise does not exist. There is no great good place, no good place that we can find; all places of our finding are in "the dominion of darkness," in the land of sin and death, and neither James nor we can do anything about sin and death. If we talk about great good places, we are writing our dreams in black ink on black walls.

There are no great good places in our world and our time. There is only a great good Person, the beloved Son of God. In Him God has dealt with our sin and our death. By His death for our sins God has "set our feet in a large room" (Psalm 31:8); He has forgiven us our sins and has ransomed us out of the dominion of darkness. He has given us the beloved Son for our Lord and King; the Son is our great good Place. This great good Place is real, as real as Bethlehem and Nazareth, as Capernaum and Nain, as Caiaphas and Pontius Pilate, as real as flesh and blood, as real as the water of Baptism, as real as the bread and wine of His Supper.

And this great good Person gives us rest, not by releasing us from pressures — who could endure a life without pressures, the pressure of the daily task for daily bread, the pressure of honorable duty, the pressure of caring for a beloved spouse, of rearing beloved children? He gives us rest by setting our messy, distraught lives in order, by laying on us the blessing of His kindly yoke — the yoke which brings with it the power to bear it and generates in us the joy that only yokebearing can give: the deep satisfaction of responsibility well met, work well done, love unstintingly given. "Come unto Me," this King says to all of us; if we will hear His voice, we shall find the great good Place.

PRAYER.

O Jesus, King most wonderful,
Thou Conqueror renowned,
Thou Sweetness most ineffable,
In whom all joys are found!

Thee may our tongues forever bless,
Thee may we love alone
And ever in our lives express
The image of Thine own. Amen.

13

Unafraid in the World

He is before all things, and in Him all things hold together.
Col. 1:17

We are all of us at one time or another afraid of the world we live in. We love this world and enjoy it; but again and again we grow afraid of it. We tremble at it even when we love it most. We read in our papers the daily record of the world's disasters: the sea, the earth, and the air all seem intent on man's destruction. We read the statistics of traffic fatalities: every car at every crossing seems destined to destroy us, and every car on every highway seems to be a missile designed for an ugly and senseless kind of slaughter. The wonderful mind of man creates the makings of a brave new world — and at the same time lets loose powers of death on a universal scale, powers that man seems helpless to control. And when we look beneath the surface of things, down into the uncanny deeps where human control stops altogether, our fear grows greater still. Our skin crawls at what we see — for we seem to see irrational powers at work, powers whose working we cannot predict or understand, powers that care nothing for our lives.

We have good reason to be afraid. We know that the earth on which we live has been cursed for our sakes; we know that this world is no longer man's world as it once was his to enjoy and to rule. This world is in fact turned against us, for the God who made it for us is turned against us. We are rebels and runaways, and we have no place to go — no place, that is, that *we* can find. But God has found a place for us, a place where we can live and be at home and safe once more. That place is the kingdom of His beloved Son. With God's Son for our King we have left the darkness of a world turned against us. We live in a world in which He is Lord, a world sustained by His gracious rule, a world which "holds together in Him." We have in Him the world as God designed it for man, for our home and our domain.

The beloved Son of God has freed our world of fear. He is our King and Lord of all the world. We know now, when we behold Him, that there is nothing accidental ever, no senseless or purposeless thing anywhere. There is no irrational evil power anywhere in our world or in our life which He does not control. No number thirteen can hurt us; no unlucky Friday can harm us. All is in the hands of the beloved Son, our King: our homes, our families, our cities, our land. We can walk confidently on the earth, for He has made the earth our inheritance (Matthew 5:5). We can sail with courage over the sea, for He has said to the sea, "Peace, be still." The beating of my heart, the drawing of my breath are part of His gracious reign over me, yes, and my growing older, too, my failing sight, my diseases, my march toward death. I can pass through the last piece of my history unafraid, for my King has said, "I am the Resurrection and the Life."

PRAYER. Give us, Almighty God, eyes to see and hearts to believe all that Thou hast given us in transferring us into the kingdom of Thy beloved Son. Teach us to live joyously and courageously in this world, which Thy love has again made ours, in Thy service and to Thy glory; through Jesus Christ, Thy Son, our Lord. Amen.

15

This Means You

And you, who once were estranged and hostile in mind, doing evil deeds, He has now reconciled in His body of flesh by His death, in order to present you holy and blameless and irreproachable before Him. Col. 1:21, 22

There is not much comfort in statistics. The worried air passenger fastening his seat belt as his plane runs into a "turbulence" (he knows it's a *storm*) cannot boost his failing courage by considering the statistical fact that a man is generally safer in a plane than he is in his home; that does not assure him that *he* is safe in *this* plane *now*. A little girl is happy and feels secure and cozy, not because she knows that fathers generally love their little girls but because *her* father showers *her* with a hundred tokens of his love.

The voice of God which reaches us in His Word is a Father's voice. It does not utter "general truths," to give us statistical security; it addresses us personally to assure us, each one of us, of His love. Paul has just set before us Christ in all His gracious glory: He is the "Image of God" (v. 15); in Him the invisible God has become present in our flesh, our history. He is Lord of all creation — "all things were created through Him and for Him" (v. 16). He is Lord of the church, united with the church as the head is united with the body (v. 18). When He died and rose again for us men, *God* was at work to reconcile all things to Himself. (vv. 19, 20)

"And *you*" — Paul funnels all this world-creating, world-sustaining, world-redeeming power and grace down directly to us. This means you. It means you, not probably and generally but you particularly and personally. This never-to-be-expected miracle, that God gave His Son into the flesh and into death for men estranged from Him, for men whose mind was set in hostility to Him, for men who documented their rebellion against Him in evil deeds — this miracle was done for you. This new creation has made a new creature of *you,* has made *you* holy, blameless, and irreproachable in God's eyes. *You* have been acquitted and set free by a Judge whose verdict no court can reverse.

The dreadful gray anonymity of the masses of men in our time, the fact that men become cogs or cards or numbers, is not the will of the God who has shown us a Father's face in Christ. *He* baptizes us individually and personally; His Son gives each of us His body and His blood in the bread and wine. He forgives us, each one, personally: *"My son . . .* your sins are forgiven." God loved the world, but He never made a cipher, a number, a statistic of anyone in the world. We who have become His dare not make statistics of men and women; if we do, we go back to that dreadful estrangement from God, that hostility to God from which Christ freed us "in His body of flesh by His death."

PRAYER. O God, let us not receive Thy grace in vain; let it live and work in each of us, where Thou hast placed us and where we stand, that each of us may be the witness of Thy love to each man who comes into our life. Give us insight into each man's need and love for all men's needs; through Jesus Christ, Thy Son, our Lord. Amen.

The Proviso of Grace

Provided that you continue in the faith, stable and steadfast, not shifting from the hope of the Gospel which you heard. Col. 1:23

"There must be a catch to it." We have all grown suspicious of anything that is "absolutely free." We have lived long enough to know that sooner or later, somehow or other, when we come to read the fine print, the free offer is not free, certainly not absolutely free. Everything costs something.

Can we believe that God's grace is absolutely free? Can we believe that the almighty and redeeming presence of God in Christ for us is free? Can we believe that the Creator Christ became one with us and died for us and made all right between our God and us — all that absolutely free? Can we believe that the deliverance which cost God the life of His Son costs us nothing? There must be a catch to it somewhere.

"Provided that you continue in the faith." Is that the catch? Does this free grace cost something after all? If we think so, we have not begun to understand Paul; we have not heard the voice of Jesus Christ, who speaks in Paul. This proviso of faith is the proviso of grace. The Giver has not suddenly become the Demander by speaking this

word "provided." The Giver is saying, "I am the Giver, and I will remain the Giver; I will be the Giver always, all the way."

For "faith" is receiving; faith is the clear-eyed recognition of *our* beggary and of God's giving. Continuing in faith means continuing in beggary before God, drawing on His riches, His strength, and His wisdom hour by hour, day by day until our days end or all days end. If we continue in faith, we continue in Him who is the Vine from whom we as His branches draw our strength and life; we cannot exist without Him. We can be "stable and steadfast" only because we are held by Him who is stable and steadfast; we hold to Him with the clutch of desperation, and *so* we are stable and steadfast too. We live under the heaven of *His* forgiveness, in the sunlight of *His* love.

His forgiveness and His love come to us in the Gospel, that mighty Word which gives what it proclaims. That Gospel holds before us the Christ who came and the Christ who shall come again. That Gospel turns our eyes toward our returning Lord and points our whole life toward His return; it makes our life even now a life of high expectancy, filled even now with the clean air of the world to come. We have that hope only in the Gospel, but we have it surely there. If we shift from the Gospel which we have heard to new gospels that turn us in upon ourselves (*our* wisdom, *our* piety, *our* high thoughts and pious speculations) we have lost our hope, our faith, our Christ. The proviso of grace is meant to save us from that; it is meant to keep the Gospel and the grace of God "absolutely free."

PRAYER. O Christ, our Strength and Hope, give us Thy gift of the Spirit that He may keep us in the faith, stable and steadfast in Thee. Amen.

Who Is Normal?

Now I rejoice in my sufferings for your sake, and in my flesh I complete what is lacking in Christ's afflictions for the sake of His body, that is, the church, of which I became a minister according to the divine office which was given to me for you, to make the Word of God fully known, the mystery hidden for ages and generations but now made manifest to His saints. To them God chose to make known how great among the Gentiles are the riches of the glory of this mystery, which is Christ in you, the hope of glory. Col. 1:24-27

"I rejoice in my sufferings" — these are amazing words, and they speak of a rare and high courage. Paul was not writing theory when he wrote them; he was a man acquainted with suffering, no stranger to imprisonments, beatings, lashes, stoning, shipwreck, dangers on land and sea. He wrote these words from prison. Neither was he indulging in hollow heroics when he wrote, "I rejoice in my sufferings." These words were soberly set down by a man who refused to boast of anything but his weaknesses, "that the power of Christ" might rest upon him (2 Corinthians 12:9), a man who said of all his strenuous labors (carried out under a severe physical handicap) that they were the work of the grace of God which was with him, a man who had no more natural taste for jails than we have — he speaks with a human and natural pathos of his imprisonment in the last verse of his Letter to the Colossians: "Remember my fetters" (4:18).

Paul shames us; we think we do well if we bear *any* suffering patiently, and the idea of suffering for others and rejoicing in it strikes us as somehow abnormal. How does one get a selfless courage like his? What is the way to this bold, defiant joy? Paul finds his joyous courage in his *"divine* office," in the fact that he is permitted "to make the Word of *God* fully known," to make known the "mystery of *Christ"* in all the riches of its glory for all men; in a word, he rejoices in suffering for the Gospel, which recounts God's great act of deliverance in Christ *and* brings that act into the lives of men as a power of God to save them.

Paul has a *divine* office; he therefore goes the way of God. That way is the way of suffering for others. Christ, the Son of God, came into the world to seek and save the lost; men do not want to admit that they are "lost," absolutely lost, and so they resist and defy Him who comes to save. Christ went through the world as a contradicted, resisted, suffering Man; His way took Him to the cross. His saving Gospel goes through the world on paths of suffering; it must, for this "mystery of Christ" robs man of all *his* glory in order to give him the one hope of glory, the Christ. Until the Gospel has gone through all time and all the world, Christ's "afflictions" will be incomplete. His *sufferings for us* and our salvation are once-for-all complete; but the "afflictions" will be there until the end of time. All who believe His Gospel and all who proclaim it may expect to endure them until the measure of these afflictions is filled up. Christ's church, His body, will in this world endure the afflictions of Christ. Paul rejoices in the fact that he is permitted to suffer for the church, that he can by his sufferings help release the power of God for all men.

Abnormal? No. It is we who shun suffering who are abnormal; we have not yet fully found wholeness and health in the one normal Man, Jesus. Because we consider suffering abnormal, we do not know the full joy of Christ. Because we will not go the suffering way of God and Christ, we have so feeble a hold on the hope of glory.

This is more easily told than learned. But let us begin to learn it; our Lord's Word holds here too: "To him who has will more be given." We need not *seek* suffering; but let us learn to greet suffering, when it comes, with the words: "Welcome, O Christ!"

PRAYER. Draw us closer to Thee, O Lord, in Thy afflictions that we may have and hold to the end the hope of glory. Amen.

Energy for the Impossible Task

Him we proclaim, warning every man and teaching every man in all wisdom, that we may present every man mature in Christ. For this I toil, striving with all the energy which He mightily inspires within me. Col. 1:28, 29

"Him we proclaim" — Paul's task as apostle of Jesus Christ is to proclaim Christ. Since Christ is Lord of all, his task is universal in scope; there is no man under the sun for whom the Christ, the Image of God, the Firstborn of all creation, Creator and Redeemer, has not died and risen again. Therefore Paul owes Him to every man; he cannot be content to create a Christian coterie, an in-group; he aims at nothing less than all men, every man; he becomes all things to all men in order that he may by all means save some. He must warn every man that in this Christ alone is life, that without Him every man is dead and gone in his trespasses and sins.

Paul's task is universal. And his task never ends. When Christ returns to judge mankind and hold the last accounting with His servants, Paul must "present every man *mature* in Christ." Therefore he must "teach every man in all wisdom"; he must open the eyes and hearts of men to the fact that Christ is Lord of their life, of all of it, of their every relationship, their every word and deed. The children whom his creative Gospel produces remain his constant care; Paul's letters are a witness to that.

The task is a staggering one — one that calls into play all Paul's energies; he "toils" and "strives." He works and sweats like any farmer or builder; he is strained and tense as an athlete running a race. He throws himself headlong and unreservedly into his task — "with all the energy" — we should expect him to go on with "all the energy *I* have." But Paul is "apostle by the will of God"; he strives with all the energy which *"He* mightily inspires." The cause of the Gospel is God's cause; *He* will make His Gospel speed and triumph everywhere; He supplies the energy, the wondrous, tireless working power that gives the speed and assures the triumph. But this does not leave room for the loveless logic which declares: "Since it is His cause and His wondrous energy at work, let Him do it." The logic of love — and all who have heard the Gospel and have been taken captive by it have been caught up in the love of God — the logic of love says: "Let me work with Thee; work Thou through me."

We who are members of the apostolic church have inherited the apostolic task: *"Him* we proclaim" to every man we meet, by everything we say and do; ours is the same unlimited, unending task. Ours is the toil and striving. Ours, too, for the asking, is all that "energy which He inspires within" those whom He has called. Christ has told us: "Apart from Me you can do nothing"; but if we do nothing, we shall be apart from Him, dead branches cut off from the vine and burned in the fire. The Christ who died for us wants *us* wholly for His own; He wants our toil and striving. Unless we toil and strive, we shall not really know Him as our Lord; we shall not know the great, the high, exhilarating energy which He inspires within the toiling, striving, believing men whom He in love has made His own.

PRAYER. Give us Thy strength that we may toil and strive for Thee, O Thou who hast toiled and striven unto death for us. Amen.

Wisdom and Knowledge

For I want you to know how greatly I strive for you and for those at Laodicea and for all who have not seen my face, that their hearts may be encouraged as they are knit together in love, to have all the riches of assured understanding and the knowledge of God's mystery, of Christ, in whom are hid all the treasures of wisdom and knowledge. Col. 2:1-3

Paul strives, with all the loving energy which God inspires in him, for the saints at Colossae, for those at Laodicea, and for all who have not seen his face — we are all included; when we read the Letter to the Colossians, we know: "This mighty apostolic Word was meant for us." Paul would have us all be "mature in Christ." Here he describes more fully the "maturity" of which he spoke before.

To be mature in Christ means two things: being knit together in love and having assured understanding and knowledge. These two, love and knowledge, do not always or even usually go together. Young people coming to a great university are often bitterly disillusioned when they get a close-up view of the mighty men of understanding and knowledge whose books they have read, whom they have worshiped from afar; these men are all too often a disappointing spectacle in their pride and pettiness, and the image of the house of knowledge is marred by their endless bitter bickerings, their ambitious and loveless scrambling for preferment, their small-souled jealousies. And we all know what the unprecedented riches of understanding and knowledge of our day have done to men and to history: they have split up the world into huge and hostile armed camps and have set man against man in murderous suspicion and hate.

But the understanding and knowledge which Paul has is of another sort entirely and has a different effect. For this is knowledge of God's "mystery," understanding of the way that God has gone through history, in ways we can understand only when He reveals them; how He has gone a way of pure, inexplicable love, to give Himself for man and to man in His beloved Son. This is knowledge and understanding of Christ, in whom we see God's face turned toward us, toward all men in forgiving grace. This knowledge is knowing that God "knows" us, chooses us and makes us His own. Knowledge is power; this understanding and knowledge is real power — the power that knits us together in love.

This is why Paul can say so sweepingly that *"all* the treasures of wisdom and knowledge" are hid in Christ and are to be found only in Christ. This does not say that all the knowledge which man has accumulated (knowledge of his world, knowledge of his fellowman, knowledge of his history) is useless and that all insight derived from this knowledge is vain. Paul's striving for us does not make us antiscientific or anticultural, or anti-anything for that matter. It is Paul who has told us, *"All things* are yours." What Paul does say is: Unless man's knowledge of the world is knowledge of the world which holds together in Christ because it was created through Him and for Him, that knowledge is fruitless and vain. Unless man's knowledge of his fellowman is knowledge of the man whom God created in His image, the man whom Christ redeemed, that knowledge is fruitless and vain. Unless his knowledge of his history is knowledge of a history which God controls and is guiding toward His great goal (the restoration of man and man's world to their ancient peace with Himself) that knowledge is fruitless and vain. For that knowledge cannot free man of his fear of the world in which he lives as an insecure alien, fear of his fellowman, fear of his future. Only in the understanding and knowledge of Christ can we have assurance; and only so can our hearts be knit together in love: love gives all knowledge its meaning and its worth.

PRAYER. Give us, O Lord, Thy Spirit to lead us into all truth; give us the Spirit of wisdom that our hearts may be knit together in love. Amen.

Sober Courage

I say this in order that no one may delude you with beguiling speech. For though I am absent in body, yet I am with you in spirit, rejoicing to see your good order and the firmness of your faith in Christ. Col. 2:4, 5

Paul is a general who must be present on all fronts; the energy which God mightily inspires in him gives him a stamina of sympathy that can reach out to all saints everywhere. Absent in body, he is present in spirit on the front in Colossae too. And he rejoices at what he sees: soldiers of Christ standing in close array and presenting a solid front. He rejoices at "the firmness of their faith in Christ."

Yet Paul is concerned for the church and toils and strives for the church at Colossae and issues a warning. He is concerned not only because of what these saints may lack; he is concerned because of what they have, because of "the firmness of their faith in Christ." And with good reason; for the enemy attacks the good work of God. *Because* Jesus was the Son of God, He had to face the tempter in the wilderness. *Because* God sows His good wheat, the enemy sows weeds on God's field. "Where God builds churches, the devil builds chapels," an old proverb has it. Where God has disclosed "all the treasures of wisdom and knowledge" in Christ, there, just there there will be a competing wisdom and knowledge. There will be *beguiling* speech by men who seek to *delude* the soldiers of Christ.

That is the great difficulty and the danger; the attack of Satan is not a frontal attack: "Satan *disguises* himself as an angel of light," and "his servants also *disguise* themselves as servants of righteousness" (2 Corinthians 11:14, 15). The solid front of massed troops does not help when the enemy infiltrates those very troops. So it was at Colossae, back in the first century: the men who tried to delude the Colossians spoke a very beguiling speech. They did not deny Christ; they only *supplemented* Him. They did not contradict the Word of truth, the Gospel; they only filled it out with strange, assorted fancies of their own. The bright, clear Christ, who gives men forgiveness and courage, Him they obscured with misty speculations that conjured up the shadow world of fear.

So it is today and will be every day until all days end. Where there is good order and firmness of faith, there will be also deluding false gospels offered with beguiling speech. We need not panic at the thought; but we must soberly face the fact that this oblique and veiled attack is an ever-present possibility. We should not underestimate the seriousness of the struggle; we are facing cunning power of darkness. But we should not be doubtful about the outcome either. We have been warned; we have the Christ and are strong in Him if we hold to Him. What is more, if Satan attacks us, he is unintentionally and unwillingly giving us high praise, for he by preference attacks the noblest works of God. There is ground for confidence and cause for courage in that.

PRAYER. We thank Thee, O Lord, for the good gifts Thou hast given us; be with us and strengthen us that no one may delude us with beguiling speech that turns us from Thee. Amen.

Just As You Were Taught

As therefore you received Christ Jesus the Lord, so live in Him, rooted and built up in Him and established in the faith, just as you were taught, abounding in thanksgiving. Col. 2:6, 7

We go stale from time to time, all of us, even the best of us. Even those blessed with a peculiarly blithe evenness of disposition in their Christian life have moments, hours, and days of bleak gloom. Our faith and hope and love go flat; the clear, rushing stream of our exuberant life in Christ dead-ends in a stagnant pool mantled with slime and smelling ill. And try as we will, we cannot fight our way out of this nightmare of dullness and despair; nothing we can do seems to help. These times are dangerous. Filled with misgiving and doubts, we are perilously open to any new beguiling speech that offers sparkling religious novelties; we are open to the infiltrations of the enemy. Paul's words to the bewildered, fumbling Christians of Colossae can help us in times like these.

These words are the first direct command in the Letter to the Colossians; and they bid us not to look about for something new but to look again at the old. They pierce our foggy gloom with three questions; if we will face and answer them, we shall find that the fog is dispelled and the gloom is gone. The first question is: Were you taught? Have you received Christ Jesus the Lord? Of course we have.

We have been baptized; our mothers and fathers brought Christ continually into our lives; the church has proclaimed Him to us in speech and song, in wood and glass and stone. We have learned our lesson; we know Him, of course.

That "of course" betrays us. There is no "of course" about this lesson ever. For we received Christ Jesus *the Lord* in that lesson. One does not learn this lesson once for all as one learns a piece of arithmetic or a rule of grammar. This introduces the second question: Have you *lived* your lesson? To learn Jesus Christ as Lord is to confess Him Lord, and to confess Him as Lord is to have Him as *your* Lord. We can learn this lesson only by living. Jesus "learned" obedience, the New Testament tells us (Hebrews 5:8); He learned obedience by obeying, by suffering in obedience to His Father's will. He lived His lesson with every human breath He drew. That sets Him apart and makes Him unique among all men who have "learned" the word and will of God. He took Scripture seriously as no rabbi ever had, and He lived it out; He beat back the tempter with three Old Testament words which thousands of Jews knew as well as He did. Let us learn the Lord, the final Word of God to us, in that same way.

We can do it; for He Himself gives us the strength to do it. We are rooted in Him; we draw life and power from Him, for we have been baptized in His name. Where there is life and power, there is growth; we are built up in Him — as He extends His Lordship ever more fully over our lives, as we "learn" the Lord more completely by living under His Lordship, we grow greater and stronger day by day. We are *"established* in *the* faith,"* the one true faith that confesses the Lord Jesus Christ. We become a tree that no winds can topple, a building that no storm can shake. We need not look around for novelties to give zest to our sodden lives; we have God's plenty in Christ Jesus, whom we have received and serve and love.

Then the third question answers itself: Have you given thanks? If we learn and live and grow and come to know how great and good His Lordship is, we abound in thanksgiving — how can we help it? The bogs and fens of doubt are far behind us, and the stream of life flows full and fresh and clear out toward the everlasting sea.

PRAYER. Give us eyes, O God, to behold the greatness and goodness of Jesus Christ our Lord that we may live under Him in His kingdom and serve Him and give Thee continual thanks. Amen.

Not According to Christ

See to it that no one makes a prey of you by philosophy and empty deceit, according to human tradition, according to the elemental spirits of the universe, and not according to Christ. For in Him the whole fullness of deity dwells bodily, and you have come to fullness of life in Him, who is the Head of all rule and authority. Col. 2:8-10

We like to think that we can, as it were, sample false religion, false teaching, false faith; that we can play around with them and take or leave them as we please, with no danger to ourselves. Paul shatters that illusion for us; there is, he tells us, an uncanny power at work in these falsities. We can take them; but we cannot be at all sure that we can leave them, for they take us. They make a prey of us, hold us fast, and destroy us.

The particular falsity which was attracting the men of Colossae called itself a "philosophy" — whether it deserved that title is another question. But it must have been impressive and intellectually respectable, a system that commended itself by its reasonable and rounded coherence. In Colossian eyes it probably "had something" or seemed to hold promise of "having something." It probably looked on the surface something like the Good News of Jesus Christ. Paul blasts its pretensions by calling it "empty deceit": it promises men fullness of truth, but it can give them only the hollowness of the lie. How could it be otherwise? For this "philosophy" led men not to Christ but to the "elemental spirits of the universe," to spiritual beings that control various portions and aspects of the world men live in and want to be secure in. These spirits, the Colossians were told by men of beguiling speech, remained a power over the Christian and threatened his existence, for the work of Christ had not dealt with them; they still needed to be reconciled, and the new philosophy was there to tell men how to deal with them and find a full and free security of life.

Christ was not being denied outright; this was a very "spiritual" philosophy and a highly "Christian" sort of human tradition. But it took a whole domain of life and removed it from the Lordship of Jesus Christ, who has reconciled *all* things to God and is "the Head of all rule and authority" — there is no power in the universe that can withdraw from His control. He, Jesus Christ, is God's full and whole and final revelation; in Him the *whole* fullness of deity dwells bodily among men; fullness of life is in Him and is given to all who believe in Him. To look out into the murky world of "elemental spirits" is to turn our backs on Him and to deny Him.

Perhaps we enlightened people of the 20th century feel superior to those poor, superstitious Colossians who could so easily be taken in by so transparent a fraud. Have we the right to feel so superior? Not so long as we still consult (half seriously or wholly seriously) astrologers and numerologists, not while we still talk of "lucky" and "unlucky" days, not while we let any power besides the Lord Jesus Christ determine our decisions, whether that power be a horoscope or something more vague and more powerful, like "the spirit of the times," "modern standards," "current practice, perfectly legal," and so on. We need Paul's key word as much as the Colossians did; perhaps we need it more, since our "elemental spirits" have so disguised themselves. That key word is: *"Not according to Christ."*

PRAYER. We thank Thee, O God, for Thy great love manifested toward us bodily in Thy Son; we thank Thee for the fullness of life which Thou hast given us in Him. Keep us, we beseech Thee, in steadfast fellowship with Him lest we become a prey to the empty deceit of false philosophies. Amen.

Forward to Christ

In Him also you were circumcised with a circumcision made without hands, by putting off the body of flesh in the circumcision of Christ; and you were buried with Him in Baptism, in which you were also raised with Him through faith in the working of God, who raised Him from the dead. Col. 2:11, 12

The search for religious novelties takes many forms. One common form is the "back to something" novelty. Men called Christians back to the Old Testament tithe or the Old Testament Sabbath. It is probably a search for security, similar to the desire to be a child again. Men think to find in ancient rites and forms a primeval simplicity and a simple, spelled-out rigor that will release them from the complexities and responsibilities of Christian freedom, that freedom which calls upon us to make decisions and to do battle on many fronts.

The men who were beguiling the Christians of Colossae were saying, "Back to the ancient rite of circumcision!" No doubt they fitted it somehow into their "philosophy" and offered persuasive arguments for falling back upon the rite which was the mark of God's ancient people, Israel. Now, circumcision had been for ancient Israel a great and precious gift of God. Paul would be the last to deny this. In circumcision God incised His gracious covenant will upon the flesh of man; with an unrepeatable act and by means of a permanent physical mark He told each male Israelite, the head of every family, "I will be your God, and I will bless you." He told it to all, slave or free, and He told it to them in their infancy; this marks this action of God as pure, undeserved grace. It is understandable, up to a point, that men should want to return to it.

But these men were ignoring one all-important fact — that when God offers Himself to us in His Son, none of His ancient blessings are lost. All are gathered up in Jesus Christ and given to us in Him. Jesus Himself has told us this. He called Himself "more than" the prophet Jonah; the Word of God that came to men of old through the prophets comes to us fuller, richer, and complete in Him. He called Himself "more than" King Solomon; the wisdom of God which once was given to Solomon is to be found in Jesus in a fullness that Solomon never knew. He called Himself "more than" the temple; God, who once was graciously present in the temple in Jerusalem, is present fully, personally, and bodily in Jesus.

And so all that circumcision ever gave to God's ancient people is present in Him too. What was a symbol and a promise in circumcision is a present, full reality in Him. In Him we are set apart as God's people; the "body of flesh," the body which expressed in action the will of our "flesh," our manhood in revolt against the God who made us — that body has been put off in Christ.

Concretely and specificially it was put off in our Baptism; there we were united with Christ, there we were incorporated in Him. In our Baptism we were united with the Christ who died for our sins and was raised up by God for our justification. We shared that death and shared the resurrection. We live as sons of Abraham, as sons of God in Him.

"Back to circumcision" is therefore no pious return to ancient sanctities; in effect it means denying Christ, God's supreme Gift to us, the Gift in which all His former gifts

37

find their fulfillment and reach their goal. We cannot go *our* ways; we can only follow in the way that God has gone; and He has gone all the way in Christ; there, in Christ, we find all the gracious and wondrous "working of God" summed up.

PRAYER. We praise and thank Thee, O God, for the inexpressible Gift of Thy Son. Keep us from foolish self-sought ways of piety, and let Thy Spirit teach us to seek and find Thee only in Thy Son Jesus Christ, our Lord. Amen.

Forgive Us Our Trespasses

And you, who were dead in trespasses and the uncircumcision of your flesh, God made alive together with Him, having forgiven us all our trespasses, having canceled the bond which stood against us with its legal demands; this He set aside, nailing it to the cross. He disarmed the principalities and powers and made a public example of them, triumphing over them in Him.
Col. 2:13-15

The whole New Testament breathes an air of bold, almost defiant confidence. It proclaims again and again and in a hundred ways: "God has acted for our salvation, and all is well!" At the same time the New Testament insists, as no other book does, on the seriousness of sin, on the guilt of man. These three verses from the Letter to the Colossians contain the New Testament Gospel in miniature, and they proclaim it with the twin emphases that are characteristic of the whole New Testament.

Every other word in these verses pronounces a curse on man the sinner. Man as the Gospel finds him is "dead in trespasses"; he has sinned against God, and God, the only Source of life, is turned against him. In the midst of life he is in death; his living heart beats out a death march, and his every breath is a dying breath. He is dead in the "uncircumcision" of his "flesh"; he is not marked out as a member of God's people, under the blessing and the prom-

39

ise of God, for he is "flesh," the creature in revolt against his Creator. There stands against him, condemning him with its demands, a huge bond of indebtedness; for man, every man, has refused to give God His due; he knows his God and yet refuses to thank and honor Him. He is like the debtor in Jesus' parable, who owes his king a debt which he cannot possibly ever pay. His sin has unleashed against him a dark host of demonic "principalities and powers" who dog his steps and fill his days and nights with nightmare fears. No doubt about it, the fact of sin is fully faced.

But if the desperateness of man confronted by his God is unsparingly told, the fact that God Himself has acted effectually and once for all in Christ is fully and triumphantly proclaimed. God has faced man's sin in all its terror and has overcome it. The Creator has made light shine out of darkness; He has made men alive again with Christ, whom He raised from the dead. God did not bypass sin, the source and cause of death; He dealt with it. He has forgiven it; He has canceled the bond of our indebtedness by paying that indebtedness Himself; He nailed the bond to that cross upon which His Son hung and cried out, "Why hast Thou forsaken Me?" and died. Thus He triumphed over the dark powers that His wrath let loose upon mankind. Now His heralds and apostles can proclaim that all is well.

God faced our sin; Christ faced our sin; the Gospel faces it. And we must learn to face it too. Our time is one in which men love to move in a dreamed-up twilight zone between right and wrong. We shrink from calling our sins by their proper names; we call them "problems" or "sicknesses" and so conceal them even from ourselves. And we wonder why we cannot find the "peace of mind" that we so ardently desire; we become like the psalmist who cried out:

> When I declared not my sin, my body wasted away
> through my groaning all day long.
> For day and night Thy hand was heavy upon me.

We have an honest God who has dealt honestly with our sin; let us come before Him honestly and confess our sins — and be forgiven for the sake of His Son, Jesus Christ, our Lord.

PRAYER.

Have mercy on me, O God,
   according to Thy steadfast love.
According to Thy abundant mercy
   blot out my transgressions. . . .
For I know my transgressions,
   and my sin is ever before me.
Against Thee, Thee only have I sinned.

Shadow Worship

Therefore let no one pass judgment on you in questions of food and drink or with regard to a festival or a new moon or a Sabbath. These are only a shadow of what is to come; but the substance belongs to Christ. Col. 2:16, 17

One of the dangerous things about false religion and false piety is that those who practice them look so overwhelmingly religious and seem so thoroughly pious that everybody is overawed by them. One feels like a cad if one does not take them at their own valuation. And so they quite naturally practice a kind of religious one-upmanship; they permit themselves sweeping judgments on everybody else's religion and piety.

The men who brought the new "philosophy" and "empty deceit" to Colossae were people of this sort. They abstained religiously from certain foods and drinks and were punctilious about observing festivals and holy days; and they put a big question mark before the piety of anyone who was not so abstinent or so liturgical as they were. "How can anyone who is really serious about his religion," they would ask, "be so careless about these things? How can they give the dark powers of evil so many opportunities to get hold of of them, these powers that lurk all over in the natural realm?" They looked down their noses at these "careless Christians" and made such an impression on at least some of the Colossian Christians that they were in danger of being trapped into this new, painfully unfree kind of piety.

Paul punctures their pretensions: "They are shadow worshipers," he says, "not worshipers of Christ." This "impressive" piety of theirs is all wrong. The ancient ordinances of God concerning food and drink and Sabbath days had their place and value in the long years in which God trained and prepared His people for the coming Christ; they wrote into the life of Israel in shadowy outline that which was to become full reality in Christ; they foreshadowed the pure people of God whom the Christ would redeem and gather and bless with rest for their souls. They have their value still as ancient witnesses to Christ (see Romans 3:21). But the substance of which they are the shadow is the Christ; He is the Body that cast those shadows. They cannot possibly be additions to Christ, supplements to Christ, or even (and this is the great and serious danger in playing with these things) *substitutes for Christ.* To cling to these things *now,* now that Christ has come, is to go our way, not God's way, for the fullness of God dwells in Christ; it is despising and refusing God's present and supreme gift, *the* gift to which these earlier gifts all pointed.

These "philosophies" and "empty deceits" have a way of turning up again and again in the life of the church, not in the same form but always with the same inhering error; they somehow want to supplement Christ and threaten to supplant Christ. A good touchstone with which to test them is this: Can I accept them and still sing, "Thou *only,* O Christ, art *most high* in the glory of God the Father"?

PRAYER. O God, who hast given us all things in Christ, let us not be turned from Him by false dreams of human piety. Amen.

The Growth That Is from God

Let no one disqualify you, insisting on self-abasement and wor-
ship of angels, taking his stand on visions, puffed up without
reason by his sensuous mind, and not holding fast to the Head,
from whom the whole body, nourished and knit together through
its joints and ligaments, grows with a growth that is from God.
Col. 2:18, 19

This is not the most vehement language concerning false
religiosity to be found in the writings of the apostle; the
Letter to the Galatians is more volcanic than this. But these
relatively calm words constitute perhaps the most damning
portrait ever drawn of the brilliant and persuasive false
teacher. He "disqualifies" the simple Christian who lives
of a simple Gospel, such as faithful Epaphras has preached
at Colossae; he creates an elite group within the church
whose members are "in" while all others are "out" or at
least pretty far out on the edge of things.

Pride is his first characteristic. But it is a "pride that
apes humility;" he distinguishes himself by self-abasement,
by being humbler than anybody — the high, courageous
boldness of men who dare call God their Father is not
found in him. Perhaps it is his humility that drives him to
worship angels; he does not dare come to God directly but
seeks Him roundabout, through His angels. This is not the
humility which God's revelation of His undeserved grace

produces in man; this "humility" feeds on the man's own visions. And therefore it is not humility at all; the man is "puffed up" over the religion which he has himself hatched out. He has no reason for pride, for it is his "sensuous mind" that has produced these religious fancies, his natural, fleshly mind that is in the last analysis always turned against God. And such is the case with this brilliant teacher's sensuous mind; he is not "holding fast to the Head" — he has loosed his hold of faith on Him who is the Image of God, the Fullness of God, the forgiving and reconciling Presence of God.

"Not holding fast to the Head" — that is the cancer that eats the heart and life out of his religion. He comes offering men "more"; more than the Gospel of Jesus Christ gave them, more than the preaching of Epaphras had given them. But he robs them of all, for he is removing them from Christ, their life. If there is to be "more" — and the Christian life is a perpetual "more," a growth and an advance — this "more" can and will come only from Him. In Him is nurture for growth, strength for unity, abundant life for *all,* for the *whole* body, not for an elite few. Any religious growth which is not growth from Him is not growth but religious suicide.

Paul did not write these words in order to make us feel complacently superior or secure. He wrote to warn us. Each of us still has an active, clever, and inventive "sensuous mind"; we all must fight the impulse to concoct sweet little religions of our own. Our hold on the Head must be perpetually renewed; and only in perpetually renewing our hold on Him, by His Word, in His Supper, shall we "grow with a growth" that is not religious cancer but the true, divine eternal "growth that is from God."

PRAYER. We thank Thee, O God, that Thou hast given Christ to be the church's Head; give us Thy strong grace that we may ever hold to Him and thus grow with the growth which is from Thee. Amen.

Take God at His Word

If with Christ you died to the elemental spirits of the universe, why do you live as if you still belonged to the world? Why do you submit to regulations, "Do not handle, Do not taste, Do not touch" (referring to things which all perish as they are used), according to human precepts and doctrines? These have indeed an appearance of wisdom in promoting rigor of devotion and self-abasement and severity of the body, but they are of no value in checking the indulgence of the flesh. Col. 2:20-23

We find it hard to take God at His word. We cannot find the heart to take the full measure of what *He* has done to us and for us in our Baptism. We men of little faith cannot wholly believe what has happened to us in Baptism and cannot confidently live the new life opened up to us by God's working. We are like a prisoner suddenly set free who cannot grasp the fact that the walls which enclosed him are no longer there, that he is free to walk anywhere in God's wide, wonderful world.

Paul's impatient questions, his two sharp whys, are designed to shake us out of this stupor of little faith and doubt and sin and to make waking, free, and joyous men of us. We have been baptized — why act as if nothing has happened? Something real and radical has happened. We have died with Christ, and that death has taken us literally and actually out of the old world in which we lived as doomed men, out of that world in which the dark, demonic powers preyed on us. Those powers can no more touch us now, no more than the police of this world can arrest and imprison a dead man.

God has acted; the thing is done. Why act as if it were not done, as if *we* must act to do it? Why act as if *we* must work our way out of the old doomed world from which God has released us? Why act as if *we* must deal with those hostile powers, when God has triumphed over them in the cross? Why try to accomplish by human precepts and doctrines, by the impotent word of men, what God's almighty Word of forgiveness has already accomplished? Why act as if we must earn the grace which God has already given us? Why pretend that we can somehow, by abstaining from this and that in a fearfully conscientious, ascetic way, do what God *has* done?

This asceticism does not make sense; but it looks as if it did. It looks like the "wisdom" whose beginning and foundation is the fear of God. This self-abasing rigor of devotion, this severe and unsparing disciplining of the body, this ascetic life, looks like that denying of oneself which Jesus asked of His disciples when He told them to take up their cross and follow Him. And yet these two are worlds apart: the renunciation which the Gospel calls for and the asceticism which the precepts of men enjoin.

Renunciation is the act of a man who turns wholly to God because God *has* turned wholly to him. As Jesus Himself describes it, it is the act of a man who, having found the one Treasure, "in his *joy*" gives up all other treasures, gladly relinquishes all second-bests for the Best.

Asceticism is the way of the man who thinks he must win God's favor, make God turn to him. It is the act of a man who refuses to believe that God has come all the way to him bodily in His Son and therefore seeks to go his own way to God. And so the ascetic must hear Paul's bitter judgment on his strenuous piety: he is really indulging the "flesh," his human, rebellious self-will, which will not take God at His Word when the Giver of the feast says: *"Everything* is ready; come to the marriage feast."

PRAYER. We thank and bless Thee, O God, for Thy full and perfect grace; make our life one great and joyous amen to the Word of forgiveness which we have heard in our Baptism, where we died to this world with Thy Son. Amen.

Lift Up Your Hearts!

If then you have been raised with Christ, seek the things that are above, where Christ is, seated at the right hand of God. Set your minds on things that are above, not on things that are on earth. Col. 3:1, 2

"Come to Me," Jesus said and offered to men, freely and without price, all that He has and all that He is. He gave men God to be their Father and Himself to be their Lord and so gave them rest for their souls. Then, when His divine grace had given men all, then and not until then He laid His gracious claim on men's lives: "Take My yoke upon you, and learn from Me."

Paul, the apostle of Jesus Christ, speaks the same language as the Lord who sent him: "With Christ you died. . . . You have been raised with Christ"; Christ has drawn you into communion with Himself; He has given Himself to you in all the glory and power and grace of His death for you and His being raised for your justification. Therefore ("If *then"),* since He has freed you from the powers of darkness and set you free for Himself, therefore give yourself to Him: "Seek the things that are above. . . . Set your minds on things that are above."

Take His yoke and let Him determine and shape your life. These "things that are above," which Paul bids us seek and set our minds on, are not some general "high ideals";

they are Christ Himself in all His gace and power for us, "Christ . . . seated at the right hand of God." Him we seek, Him we set our minds on, the Christ who lived for us, who died for us, who reigns in all the might and majesty of God for us, Lord over all and forever.

If we seek Him, then, we seek Him as our Lord; we would be His servants, doing His will in the power He can give us. This means quite simply that we live His life of love — love for God and love for man is unbroken unity; that we set our mind on living for others, for the men and women and children whom God has set beside us and around us in the world. It means following in the footsteps of Him who came to minister, who expended Himself in glorifying His Father by giving Himself recklessly and unstintingly for men, for His own and for His enemies.

"Set your minds . . . *not* on things that are on earth." On this earth this kind of life is lived against the grain, against the constant, overwhelming pressure of the majority who seek their own. Over against this one Voice that bids us live for others there are a thousand voices that persuade us, urge us, and entice us to live for ourselves, to get and to enjoy all we can while we can. We can go against the grain only in the power which comes to us from Christ, who is at the right hand of God. That power does come to us, in His Word, in the bread and wine of His Supper, in which He gives us nothing less than Himself, His bodily self that lived and died for us.

This is all very general; we should like specifics. We want to be told *how* to live this triumphant life of love in all the details of our life, in every situation. And Paul will give us specifics too; we shall find the apostolic word embarrassingly pointed and explicit before we have done with Paul's Letter to the Colossians. But unless we hear and heed this very general Word and resolutely give our will and thoughts to our enthroned Lord, we shall labor drearily at the specifics and never know how joyous and courageous a thing the life lived in Christ can be.

PRAYER. Thy voice, O Lord, Thy mighty voice, has spoken in Thine apostle and has bidden us: "Lift up your hearts!" Give us Thy Spirit that we may give the answer of faith: "We lift them up unto the Lord." Amen.

The Hidden Glory

For you have died, and your life is hid with Christ in God. When Christ, who is our Life, appears, then you also will appear with Him in glory. Col. 3:3, 4

"We behold His glory," John the Evangelist says of the life of Christ on earth. What kind of glory was that? It was the glory of the Lamb of God that dies for the sins of the world, the glory of the Good Shepherd who dies for His sheep that they may have life and have it more abundantly, the glory of the Crucified. It was the glory of a perfect love, a glory which only the eyes of faith could see. What kind of glory does the Son of God have now? His glory is not manifest in the church, which is His body; and it is not manifest in the world over which He rules. It is a hidden glory now, "hid . . . in God." The only glory of the enthroned Christ is the glory of His love, a glory which only those who are loved by Him and love Him know and can adore.

Christ is our Life. "It is no longer I who live, but Christ, who lives in me; and the life I now live in the flesh I live by faith in the Son of God, *who loved me and gave Himself for me,*" Paul says elsewhere. Our life, too, is a hidden life: it is hidden with Christ, the Son of God, who loved us and gave Himself for us. Therefore the only glory of our life, too, is a hidden glory, the unspectacular glory of the love that gives itself for others. That is the only glory which the church may look to have on earth.

But the glory of Christ is hidden *in God;* and nothing hidden with Him is ever lost or destroyed. Jesus Himself has said, "Nothing is covered that will not be revealed, or hidden that will not be known." The hidden glory of the Servant Christ will break forth for all to see: every knee shall bow to Him, and every mouth shall confess Him as Lord. We know and confess, "And He shall come again with glory to judge both the quick and the dead." If our life is hidden with Him in God, we know (and this is the most certain of certainties in our life) that we, too, shall appear with Him in glory. The life which we have committed to God, the glory which we have put in His keeping, are in safekeeping.

If we seek that which is above, we at the same time seek and strain toward that which is to come; we are tensed toward glory as we pray, "Maranatha — our Lord, come." This puts a wondrous blessing on our life; it gives us a detachment from this world which enables us to fill our life more fully with its hidden glory of love. "Detachment," however, is a cool word and does not altogether express what should be said. This "detachment" is not the cool, intellectual detachment of the philosopher; rather it is like the detachment which comes upon a man when he is about to leave forever a town in which he has lived for many years. He finds that he loves his friends more generously than he did before; their faults and shortcomings no longer seem important. Old irritations no longer have the power to irritate him. Old competitions and frictions no longer move him. As he takes his last walk through the old, familiar streets, a golden and benevolent calm comes over him.

PRAYER. We thank Thee, O God, for the hidden glory of our lives. Give us, we pray, the patience which can endure the hiddenness in the sure hope of the glory to come. Amen.

A Choice of Deaths

Put to death therefore what is earthly in you: immorality, impurity, passion, evil desire, and covetousness, which is idolatry. On account of these the wrath of God is coming. Col. 3:5, 6

We have no choice about death: we must die. But we have a choice of deaths, and we must make the choice. We must choose between death now or death later. Paul is speaking of "death later" when he says, "On account of these the wrath of God is coming." Until the wrath of God comes, man is free — free to live it up in immorality, impurity, passion, evil desire, free to make things his god, free to worship mammon if he wills. But he will find that living it *up* has been the very opposite of what he thought it was; he will find that he has lived it *down* — down to the depths of eternal *dying.* For the wrath of God will not annihilate him; he will not escape into nothingness: the wrath of God will judge him and separate him forever from his God, from life and joy. The warmth and splendor and full fellowship of God's eternal feast will not be his; he shall have instead the agony of being eternally shut out, consigned to what Jesus called the outer darkness, where there is weeping and gnashing of teeth.

The other choice is death now, death by Baptism into the death of Christ. That death means that we have died to the power of sin, which rules mankind; it means that we have been released from the intolerable slavery to sin, that power which pays the due wages, death, to all its servants. It means that now, in this life, we are called upon to do battle with that power which still besets us and seeks to enslave us again; it means a battle to the death with immorality, impurity, passion, and evil desire. It means serving and loving God alone, with a resolute turning away from the idol mammon. It means putting to death covetousness, that sin which appears in so many respectable forms and assumes such fine sentimental disguises: "the good life"; "a decent standard of living"; "you owe it to yourself"; "you owe it to your family"; "security" — to mention just a few. It means the daily *life* of repentance of which Luther spoke in that sentence which ushered in the Reformation.

This is a battle we can fight and fight successfully only because we have died with Christ — and have risen with Him, too, and now share His life as the Risen One. That is the meaning of Paul's "therefore": because God has brought you through death into life, *therefore* live that new life; live it as an amen to God's Word of forgiveness, as a doxology in action to Him who loved us and gave Himself for us. This is what Jesus said to us when He said: "He who finds his life will lose it, and he who loses his life for My sake will find it."

That is His word to us; that is His inexpressible gift to us, this possibility of death for His sake now, and hereafter life with Him forever. The threat of the wrath of God, a real and serious threat, is not meant to make whimpering cowards of us; that threat is kept before us in order that the fear of God may drive out every other fear and make us hold in joyous desperation to Him who is our Life.

PRAYER. We thank Thee, O Lord, for the gift of Baptism; give us grace to live daily in our Baptism that we may put to death all that is earthly in us and, fearing Thee, be freed of every fear. Amen.

The Dreadful Alternative

In these you once walked when you lived in them. But now put them all away: anger, wrath, malice, slander, and foul talk from your mouth. Do not lie to one another, seeing that you have put off the old nature with its practices and have put on the new nature, which is being renewed in knowledge after the image of its Creator. Col. 3:7-10

Paul's letters were written to young churches, to men and women who came to faith and were baptized as adults; for these readers their pagan past was a vivid and painful memory. They knew firsthand what life without Christ, life outside Baptism is like; they knew what is at stake in the Christian life, what a lapse from faith and a denial of their Baptism would mean for them. It is good for us who were baptized as infants to read the words with which Paul recalls this evil past, this dark time before their Baptism. It brings home to us the blessing of our Baptism, what we have been spared by being brought to Christ as little children. We see how dark and dreadful the alternative to the life of the baptized is. And we realize afresh how seriously we must take the imperative, the "should," of Baptism which we know from our Catechism; we realize that it is a matter of life or death "that the Old Adam in us *should* by daily contrition and repentance be drowned and die with all sins and evil lusts and again a new man daily come forth and arise, who shall live before God in righteousness and purity forever."

The alternative to a life built on Baptism is pictured by Paul in the words, "In these [sins] you once walked when you lived in them." Men not only *walk* in sins; sins are not only the surroundings and circumstances of their life, not only incidents in their history. They *live* in sins; their life history and their life element is sin, a helpless, hopeless, constant rebellion against their God. And this rebellion against God works itself out in man's relationship to man also, in anger, wrath, malice, slander, foul talk, and the lie. Man turned against his God is turned against his fellowman also and seeks to ruin him.

From this we have been delivered; to this we shall return if we do not daily put away all that threatens our new life as baptized men, as men who have put on the new nature. And we *can* put away all that threatens us; we need not walk in sins or live in sins. God *has* dealt with us and has clothed us with the new nature. God has given us His Son, the Image of the invisible God; through His Son, through our Baptism, which united us with the Son, He has brought us back to the world's first bright days, when man was created in the image of God. Through Him God has made us again in His image. We stand before God as Adam stood, in free converse and communion with God, rulers of the world, obedient and responsible to God in our dominion; all things are ours. And what God has done in Baptism He continues to do: He renews us constantly after His own image, the image of the Creator. We are being renewed "in knowledge." As we come to know our God better and better through His Word, we are renewed as the new creation of God, as men in Christ. We take another step, however hesitant and faltering — a short step, perhaps, but a step — a step toward Paradise.

PRAYER. Renew us, O God, in knowledge of Thee that we may walk and work in love as men created in Thine image through Thy Son. Amen.

Integration

Here there cannot be Greek and Jew, circumcised and uncircumcised, barbarian, Scythian, slave, free man, but Christ is all and in all. Col. 3:11

The life of the new man, the man re-created in Christ after the image of his Creator, is lived in a community. It is by nature and by definition a life lived in the fellowship of the church just as surely as it is a life built on Baptism. "For by one Spirit we were all baptized into one body," the body of Christ, the church. There, in the church, we find the power and inspiration for a life lived for others; for there the Word of Christ dwells richly; there the Lord gives Himself to us in His Supper in the bread and wine. There "Christ is all and in all."

There each man can be a Christ to his neighbor, as Luther put it; there he can serve his neighbor, call him to repentance when he sins, and forgive him and restore him. There the strong can help and build up the weak; there the wise can counsel the simple; there the rich can help the poor. There all the gifts of the Spirit find full play and can be put to God's uses. There Christ is all. And there Christ is in all. I find Christ in my brother's word to me, in that precious and homely form of the Gospel which Luther called "the mutual converse and consolation of the brethren." Christ meets me in my brother's need of me; there I can serve my Lord by simple ministries to the least of His brethren.

Therefore it follows as the night the day that "here there cannot be" any of the divisions created by differences in race or history or social status or culture. These lines of division simply fade away in the church; they are wiped out by the great and overruling fact of Christ. They may continue in the world; the Christian slave may remain a slave even if he has a Christian master. Paul was sending a runaway Colossian slave, Onesimus, back to his master with the bearer of his Letter to the Colossians. But in the church he is a free man among men set free by Christ; the fact that he is a slave simply does not count. He is a "faithful and beloved brother," no less.

We cannot read these lines without thinking of our snug little parishes in "nice" sections of the city; they make no rules to keep anybody out, to be sure. But how is it that the not-so-nice people from not-so-nice sections never get in? How is it that these nice parishes remain so uniformly nice year after year — or relocate when the niceness of the neighborhood begins to wear thin?

We cannot but think of segregation when we read these lines. That word "segregation" is a particularly nasty word in a Christian's mouth, for the root meaning of the word is "separation from the *flock*." We are resisting and denying the one Good Shepherd of us all when we segregate the Negro or anybody else; for He has said, "There shall be one flock, one Shepherd." The Negro has been imprisoned by stouter walls than walls of brick or stone; unless we find our way to him and unless we let Christ be all and in all, black or white, we must fear that one day we shall hear the Lord Christ say, "I was . . . in prison, and you did not visit Me."

PRAYER. We thank thee, O God, for the gift of Thy grace to all men. Give us the heart and the wisdom to let Christ be all in all and to see Him and love and serve Him in all our brethren. Amen.

New Clothing

Put on then, as God's chosen ones, holy and beloved, compassion, kindness, lowliness, meekness, and patience, forbearing one another and, if one has a complaint against another, forgiving each other; as the Lord has forgiven you, so you also must forgive. And above all these put on love, which binds everything together in perfect harmony. Col. 3:12-14

Loving "everybody" is easy. It is not too hard to be compassionate, kind, lowly, meek, and patient toward people in general and at a distance, toward people whom we never see and probably will never meet. We pray for the conversion of our enemies, send a check to Lutheran World Relief, make out another for missions, commend all men to the everlasting mercies of God, and go about our daily business with a tolerable opinion of ourselves. The five nouns which Paul lists as the garments, or armor, that a Christian should wear as his daily dress and equipment do not particularly shame us; we can check them off one by one and feel that we have not scored too badly in the test.

We should love everybody; that belongs to the ABCs of our faith. But (and this is where we comfortably deceive ourselves) we have not loved everybody until we love the people we meet every day or every week. Here is where we are really put to the test, when we are called upon to "forbear *one another*" and to "forgive *each other*" when it comes to hard, concrete, close, and individual cases. What becomes of our compassion, kindness, lowliness, meekness, and patience when we are called upon to forbear the person who is always wrong and always insists that he is in the right, the stupid, vain, disagreeable, meddling, fussy man who makes every committee meeting an agony, twice as long as it would have to be and intolerably inefficient? Do we forbear *him* — or do we ride over him? Do we forgive him his faults in meekness and humility — or do we feel superior and harsh toward him as we say, "There he goes again"?

Then we realize our bankruptcy in all these glorious Christian qualities; then we come to know again, to our shame, that this compassion and this kindness and all the rest are not flowers that grow in our garden, that they are never qualities that we "have." We know they must be constantly given us by the God whose wholly undeserved mercy has made us His own — He chose us in the free graciousness of His love; He made us "holy," His own choice possession; we are His beloved because He first loved us.

We must "put on" compassion; it must be given us. We can be compassionate only by letting the compassion of Christ fill us and spill over from us to the man beside us. Our kindness, if it be real kindness, is but the reflection of the kindness which God has shown us in Christ. We can go the way of humility and meekness and patience with our fellowman only because Jesus has gone that way before us and for us and because He lives in us and does *His* gracious work through us. We can forgive, really forgive, because He has forgiven us, because *we* live entirely of His forgiveness. We can put on the love that binds all these golden qualities together into a perfect, functioning whole, the love that binds men together into the church that does Christ's work, only because God has rent the heavens and come down to us in His Son with a love that loved the world.

PRAYER. We thank Thee, O Lord, for all the blessings of Thy love; let Thy love live and work in us that we may forbear and forgive each other as Thou hast forgiven us. Amen.

Controlling Atmosphere

And let the peace of Christ rule in your hearts, to which indeed you were called in the one body. And be thankful. Col. 3:15

There are places in the world, by the sea, in a virgin forest, on great plains, in the mountains, beside clear streams, where one can only be silent; there is that in the air which forbids speech. There are grave and stately streets in old cities which compel us to walk decorously; there can be no sauntering or whistling here. There are little village streets down which you cannot hurry; without thinking, you slow your pace. There are noble buildings in which you instinctively do not raise your voice; loud talk or laughter would be incongruous there. We all recall how the homes in which we grew up shaped and restrained our conduct; certain things were simply not done within their walls. Some powerful combination of elements that we never stopped to analyze constituted a *controlling atmosphere* which ruled in our hearts.

This "controlling atmosphere" is a weak comparison for what the peace of Christ is or should be in our lives. What is this "peace of Christ"? The prophet Isaiah was permitted to look down the long corridors of the centuries to the birth of Christ; he called the hoped-for, longed-for Child the Prince of Peace. And his prophecy made plain what he meant by "peace": the light of God's new creation breaking upon men walking in a land of deep darkness, glory for contempt, joy as joy at harvesttime when men rejoice in God's good gifts, the breaking of the rod and yoke of the oppressor, an end to the futile, bloody agony of war, a reign of justice and of righteousness forevermore.

When the Child was born, the angels sang, "Peace on earth"; the life and work of the Christ made clear what this peace meant: "Son, your sins are forgiven"; and all the ruination which sin has wrought is overcome — the lame walk, the blind see, the lepers are cleansed, the ruinous demons are cast out. All is well and sound and whole again; all is divinely normal again, man and man's world are made fresh and clean and bright as they came from the Creator's hand. It is a costly thing, this peace of Christ: it cost the blood of Christ. God made "peace by the blood of His cross." (Colossians 1:20)

The Gospel is the Gospel of peace, for it gives us Christ, who is our Peace. This powerful Word called us into the peace of Christ, that peace which only God can give and we can only receive from Him. We were called into peace "in the one body"; this controlling atmosphere of peace is alive and powerful. It gives us work to do and gives us the strength to do it. No member of the body is an idle member; in a healthy body all members function; they do the work they are designed to do.

It is essential to the health of the body and of every part of the body that the peace of Christ *rule*. The atmosphere of peace, the wholeness and health which God has given us in Christ, is by nature a ruling and controlling reality. But it can be resisted, and we men of flesh and blood do blindly and madly resist it. Therefore we must hear the apostolic word: *"Let* the peace of Christ rule in your hearts." Let this atmosphere determine whether you may think this thought, speak this word, do this deed — can this be done in this atmosphere? How shall I, in this enveloping and controlling atmosphere of the peace of Christ, bear this weakness, this illness, this bereavement? These are all-important questions, for unless we live in this atmosphere and let it rule in our hearts, we leave that life-giving air for the fatal fogs of death. If we let it rule, our lives will be bold, full, vigorous lives, filled with the music of thanksgiving.

PRAYER. O Prince of Peace, keep us and guide us on the paths of peace, and make us thankful. Amen.

The Singing Apostolic Church

Let the Word of Christ dwell in you richly as you teach and admonish one another in all wisdom and as you sing psalms and hymns and spiritual songs with thankfulness in your hearts to God. Col. 3:16

"And I believe one holy Christ and *apostolic* church," we confess with all Christendom in the Nicene Creed. There is hardly a sentence in the New Testament which sums up so briefly and precisely what "apostolic church" means as this word of Paul's in Colossians 3:16. Paul here describes the activity of the church in almost precisely the same words he used to describe his own mission as apostle (1:28). "Him [Christ] we proclaim," he says of himself. "Let the Word of Christ dwell in you," he says of the church. "Warning and teaching every man," he says of himself. "Teach and admonish one another," he says of the church. The apostle and the apostolic church have the same basis in Christ and perform the same task, and they both do it in the same way: "in all wisdom." The apostolic church lives of the apostolic Word and carries on the apostolic task; the apostolic church is the church in which the apostolic Word dwells, works, and sings.

"Let the Word of Christ dwell in you richly." Where the Word of Christ is, where the apostolic Word is, there the apostolic church is, there the sheep of God's pasture hear the voice of the Good Shepherd and are united by that voice. Therefore the word must *dwell* among us, a permanent guest among us from the world of God. When the Word leaves, the church ceases to be. And it must dwell "richly" in fulness and in many forms so that it can permeate the whole life of the church and the life of each man in the church. We should never grow too old for our Catechism and should never cease to thank God for it; but the Catechism was never designed to be a substitute for the full riches of the Word of Christ. Unless we let the Catechism drive us into the Word and be our guide through the Word in all its riches, we have not used our Catechism rightly.

The Word of Christ must dwell among us; and since it is a lively, powerful, working Word, it cannot but work among us. That Word will make us wise in the one wisdom that counts: it will give us insight into God's way with us and His will for us. In the strength of that Word we can teach one another; we can speak the Word which will let Christ grow great before our eyes in all His gracious majesty. And a teaching of Christ will always be an admonishing of one another. We cannot, for instance, speak of the Christ who fed the 5,000 without saying, "This means you" — you with your worries about feeding your family, about security for your old age. We cannot speak of the Crucified to one another without saying to one another, "This means you" — you who cannot sleep because your conscience troubles you. We cannot speak of the Christ who said, "Follow Me," without calling upon one another to turn from all that distracts and tempts us and to follow Him in singleness of heart. And what a wealth of means our God has given us in this our day, means for teaching and admonishing one another throughout the length and breadth of Christendom: printing, radio, television, audio-visual aids!

Where the Word dwells richly, there will be music; we grow strong and bold from our daily diet of the potent Word. The Spirit moves us mightily to sing inspired song.

> The church with psalms *must* shout;
> No door can keep them out.

We cannot hire this singing done for us; this we must do ourselves, not leave it to a few experts. We will use the experts in verse and music gratefully, those men of all tongues and all ages whose best songs fill our hymnals; but singing is our own high and holy apostolic task, one that we cannot shuffle off. In so high a ministry small things become important. Neither God nor the church of God cares whether you sing *well* or not; but God cares whether you sing with thankfulness in your heart or not. And unless you take seriously the fact that your singing is an apostolic ministry to the church, the church of God will suffer for it; some little one whom God has put beside you may perish for lack of the Word that you, just you, might have sung to him, teaching and admonishing him.

PRAYER. We thank Thee, O God, for the riches of the apostolic Word; give us, we pray Thee, grace to let it work among us and wisdom to speak it to our fellowman. Amen.

In the Name of the Lord Jesus

And whatever you do in word or deed, do everything in the name of the Lord Jesus, giving thanks to God the Father through Him. Col. 3:17

Paul armors us for action with a coat of triple brass. He has spoken of the *peace* of Christ which rules in our hearts and of the *Word* of Christ which dwells in us richly. Now he speaks of the *name* of the Lord Jesus: "Do everything in the *name* of the Lord Jesus." The name is of importance in the language of the Bible; the name of God or the name of Jesus signifies not merely who He is but *what* He is, what He signifies for us; the "name" of Jesus is Jesus turned toward us as Savior and Lord. If we speak or act "in the name of the Lord Jesus," that means: His name is spoken over every word and deed of ours; we call upon Him, and we point to Him and say: *"He* is the Author of each good and kindly word I speak; He is the Doer of my every gracious deed."

Of what sort must these words and deeds be that the name of the Lord can be truly spoken over them, that they can be called fruit borne by branches which draw their life and power from the Vine? Paul here calls Him simply by His human name, Jesus; he is looking back to the days when the Son of God walked the earth with us. What were the words and deeds of Jesus like?

In word and deed He sought the glory of His Father. He

willed to live by every word that proceeds from the mouth of God; His meat was to do the will of the God who sent Him and to accomplish His work. He sought to make men bow in adoration and love before the God who alone is good, who is wholly good. He could say at the close of His life, "Father . . . I glorified Thee on earth." He went in free obedience into death and took the bitter cup from His Father's hand that God's grace and righteousness might prevail. Any deed done in His name must be free of selfish ambition for our own glory; the Lord Jesus has bidden us let our light shine before men that men may see our good works and glorify our Father who is in heaven.

In word and deed Jesus won His victory over the enemy of God. He met the satanic temptation clear-eyed and unafraid, clinging to the Word of God, which was for Him the voice of His Father. He entered the house of the strong man, Satan, bound him, and plundered him of his goods by driving out the Satan's powers which ruled ruinously over men possessed by them. Any deed done in His name will be done with a whole *no* to the satanic power; it will be done without compromising with the satanic lie, without submitting to the satanic delusion that one can serve both God and oneself.

In word and deed He lived a life devoted wholly to others. He came to seek and save the lost, to be a Servant to mankind. He expended Himself in ministry and crowned a life of ministry by giving His life as a ransom for many. Any deed done in His name must be a deed of love, of love active in a ministry for others.

Then all our life will be one eloquent thanksgiving to God. Our deeds as well as our words will be an utterance of thanks "through Him" who has given us all the good gifts of God, who made us sons of God who give God a son's obedience and praise Him with a child's glad, grateful heart.

PRAYER. Lord Jesus, give us the Spirit which Thou hast promised to Thine own that all our words and deeds may be a great thanksgiving uttered in Thy name. Amen.

God's Word to Wives and Husbands

Wives, be subject to your husbands, as is fitting in the Lord. Husbands, love your wives, and do not be harsh with them.
Col. 3:18, 19

"Be subject." These words have no popular appeal. Thinking men who get their norms and standards from the world of men will dismiss them, no doubt, as ignoring a woman's basic rights as a human being; and unthinking people, who instinctively pick up their standards from what everybody is saying, will be repelled by them; they are unromantic, undemocratic, and (apparently) unrealistic words. Even Christians find this a hard saying, and one can read clever and learned comments by Christian scholars on this passage which manage to make Paul say something that he did not say and evade what Paul very obviously did say. Uncomfortable words, these.

What shall we make of them? First of all, let us hear Paul out. Paul does not speak of *anybody's* rights in marriage, either the husband's or the wife's. If he bids wives be subject, he does not tell the husbands to rule but to love; and he uses the same word for "love" here that Jesus used when He said, "God so *loved* the world that He *gave*"; the same word that he himself used in his great chapter on love in his First Letter to the Corinthians. He is speaking of that self-giving, self-sacrificing love which "is patient and kind . . . is not jealous or boastful . . . is not arrogant or rude . . . does not insist on its own way . . . is not irritable or resentful . . . does not rejoice at wrong but rejoices in the right . . . bears all things, believes all things, hopes all things, endures all things." No less than this is required of the Christian husband as head of the family: he is to live wholly and always for the woman whom God has given him, with a love like God's own self-sacrificing love.

To such a man the wife is told to subject herself in order to receive his love, to live her life in free self-giving to a spouse whose love for her is a reflection of the love of God, who called Himself the Husband of His chosen people, to describe His love for them. She is to be to her husband what the church is to Christ. Hers is the most "churchly" of all human vocations; and his is the most "Christly" of all human lives, for he is to be to her what Christ is for the church. Thus the wife's subjection is "fitting in the Lord"; it is her divinely appointed way of seeking the things that are above, where Christ is at the right hand of God. It is her worship, just as her husband's love for her is his worship.

There is a risk in this. The Christian woman lays her whole life into the hand of her spouse, for better or for worse. This being subject calls for the highest kind of Christian courage — at the beginning of marriage and throughout marriage. Not all husbands are loving, and no loving husband is always and without exception loving. The Christian husband takes over an awesome responsibility when he says, "I take thee"; he must needs have a stout and resolute love; for not all wives subject themselves, and no wife is always the wife she should be "as is fitting in the Lord." All spouses live of each other's forgiveness. But if there is a risk in Christian marriage, the risk is graver in any other kind, one which substitutes *our* wisdom regarding man and woman for the loving wisdom of our God. The rebellious woman and the harsh and tyrannous man have both corrupted their lives at life's heart and core, in its relation to God. What marriage counseling of a secular sort can restore to health and wholeness such a life? And how shall a marriage ruined by such a life be renewed?

PRAYER. We thank Thee for the blessing of marriage, O God; give us grace to live in this holy estate in free obedience to Thy will, as is fitting in the Lord. Amen.

Lordly Parents

Children, obey your parents in everything, for this pleases the Lord. Fathers, do not provoke your children lest they become discouraged. Col. 3:20, 21

There is nothing particularly original about these words; any pagan moralist might have written them, and many a pagan moralist has written very similar words — except for one thing, the basic motive for the child's obedience: "for this pleases the Lord." The child's obedience is his service to the Lord Jesus Christ, through whom the world was made, in whom all things hold together; service to Him in whom we have redemption, the forgiveness of sins, to Him who shall appear in glory at the end of days. The child's obedience to his parents is his act of faith in the Lord who died for Him. The child's obedience is his worship, his sacrifice of thanksgiving and praise.

This kind of obedience cannot be compelled or forced upon the child. It must be inspired. That is why Paul does not tell the fathers they are to rule over their children (that is obvious) but instead warns them not to irritate or provoke their children "lest they become discouraged" and their obedience becomes an unhappy, forced, and joyless way of getting by. That kind of obedience cannot please the Lord.

This puts a great burden of responsibility on fathers. We must *inspire* obedience in our children; and there is no set of rules to teach us that. We each of us must *be* the sort of man in whom the child beholds his Lord: Christ must shine through us in our sternest and in our mildest moments. The child must see in our face that which he would fain call Master, that which impels him inwardly to give his life into our hands freely and gladly, knowing instinctively that his life will be guarded, tended, cherished, and fostered there.

Who is sufficient for these things? Not one of us so long as we seek this sufficiency in ourselves or in the dozens of books on child rearing which never speak of the Lord. We must seek our sufficiency in Him. We must seek and set our minds on things that are above, on Christ the Lord seated at the right hand of God, and let His love and authority shine through us; we must put to death what is earthly in us and resolutely put off the old nature and put on the new, the man created in Christ after the image of God.

We must put on all that becomes us "as God's chosen ones, holy and beloved": compassion (how genuine compassion inspires confidence and obedience in the child!) kindness, lowliness and meekness (a haughty father can enforce obedience, but he cannot inspire the glad obedience which makes the happy child), and the patience which can forbear and forgive (where will the little child learn that God is the great Forgiver if he does not learn it from the love of his forgiving father?), and love that makes a gracious whole of all our several kindnesses. The peace of Christ, the Word of Christ, the name of Christ — these must be the power that rules benignly over us; thus they can also rule through us and help us put the gentle yoke of Christ upon the child.

This does not exclude firmness and discipline. Indeed, they are demanded, for the Christ is firm with us and disciplines us; and the weak, indulgent father provokes and discourages his children as much as the harsh and haughty one. But children have a sure sense, or instinct, for love even when love is concealed in sternness. If the peace of Christ rules our rebukes and punishments, the child will sense that peace of Christ unerringly — and bless us for our firmness when he grows into a man.

PRAYER. We thank Thee for the privilege of fatherhood, O Father; give us grace and wisdom so to rear our children that they find Thy love in us. Amen.

Slaves of the Lord Christ

Slaves, obey in everything those who are your earthly masters, not with eyeservice, as menpleasers, but in singleness of heart, fearing the Lord. Whatever your task, work heartily, as serving the Lord and not men, knowing that from the Lord you will receive the inheritance as your reward; you are serving the Lord Christ. For the wrongdoer will be paid back for the wrong he has done, and there is no partiality. Col. 3:22-25

What does a word spoken to slaves, even if it be an apostolic word, mean to us, to free men in a free society? Two things at a minimum.

First, it brings home to us in a peculiarly concrete and striking way how seriously we are to take the fact that God is Lord of *all* history and that *all* things hold together in Christ. If ever a man was not consulted about his history, the ancient slave was that man. If he had ever been free, having come into slavery by capture in manhood, his past was a book slapped shut, never to be opened again. His present was absolutely out of his control; he was completely at the disposal and under the control of the man who owned him; even so enlightened a Greek as the philosopher Aristotle could speak of the slave as "an animated tool." As for his future — it could happen that a kindly master set free a faithful slave; but in general the slave's future was as gray and hopeless as his present.

And yet Paul expected of the slave no less a faith than this: that he believe that God Himself had put him where he was and that he was to serve the Lord Jesus Christ just there, in that gray anonymous lot of his, as an animated tool in another's hand. This lets a blast of cool and wholesome air into our steam-heated lives, our feverish dreams of getting more and more and more, our fretful frustrations, our impatience with the narrow stage the God of history has given us to tread upon. Serve Him there, little man, just there, and be content. God knows where He wants you, and His love has set you there.

The second thing is this: We *are* free, and we should thank God for that blessing. But none of us is wholly free; all of us who work for a living are part-time slaves, under set terms, of course, and free (to a degree, at least) to change masters or to seek better terms. Our slavery is a distant relative, but a relative, to the slavery of the ancient slave; and all the light which Paul's Gospel shed on the servitude of the slave falls on our service too. We, too, are at bottom not serving merely men but the Lord; our every piece of dull and deadening work is done for Him. And this transfigures all the work we do — it becomes a piece of grateful worship, an adoration of the Lord.

The Gospel transfigures our present task; and it opens up a great future. We work for the Lord; no man deserves a reward from Him, for He has given and gives us all things. But such is His lavish, generous grace that no one who works for Him goes unrewarded: "From the Lord you will receive the inheritance as your reward." "The inheritance" — that means eternal life, the Kingdom, God's blessing; that means that God will dwell among us and that we shall be His people, that He shall wipe all tears forever from our eyes, that death and mourning, cry and agony shall be no more, that we shall see Him face to face in a world made new by His creative Word.

If we give ear to the assurance and the promise of Jesus Christ in the words of His apostle, we must hear his exhortation too: "Obey in everything" — no selective service here! "Not with eyeservice, as menpleasers" — the boss's eye may not be on us, but the eye of the Lord Jesus is. "Work heartily" — no work we do for the Lord can seem meaningless; if it is His will, it is worth doing, and we can throw ourselves into it.

And we must hear the apostolic warning too: "The wrongdoer will be paid back for what he has done, and there is no partiality." The Lord will not ask whether we were big men or little men, whether the work we were doing seemed to us worthwhile or not. He will ask only one thing of us all: "You were My servant; did you do My will?"

PRAYER. We thank Thee, O Lord, that Thou hast set us free and hast made us Thy servants in all that we do. Give us grace to work heartily for Thee. Amen.

Five Marks of Prayer

Continue steadfastly in prayer, being watchful in it with thanks-giving; and pray for us also, that God may open to us a door for the Word, to declare the mystery of Christ, on account of which I am in prison, that I may make it clear as I ought to speak. Col. 4:2-4

"Lord, teach us to pray," the disciples entreated Jesus. Paul is an apostle of Jesus Christ; Jesus Christ speaks in him, and Jesus' teaching on prayer is continued through him. Paul here gives us five marks, or tokens, of prayer; by them our praying can be tested (and be found wanting, no doubt) and be corrected and encouraged and shaped and guided. Our praying is to be steadfast, watchful, thankful, for others, and for the cause of God.

"Continue steadfastly in prayer." Happy the man who does not need this reminder and is not shamed when he puts his praying to the test suggested by Paul's command. Most of us must look back in shame and penitence on long stretches of our life in which prayer was sparse and mechan-ical or completely absent. We grow weary in praying or lose heart; and the less we pray, the less heart we find for praying. We forget how totally we depend on our Father in heaven, and our life becomes a gray and sweating grind, cheerless and hopeless.

Steadfastness in prayer does not necessarily mean long prayers, but it does mean praying at every turn of the road: when we awake and when we go to sleep, before and after meals — that much is self-evident for most of us. But if that is all, we have not really learned to pray. Do we pray when we get behind the wheel of our car and take all that power into our hands? Have we experienced the blessing of that fine old custom of praying our way through our Bibles or through the old familiar Catechism, pausing for converse with the Lord as we finish a section or a chapter? Do we pray before meeting difficult people who are going to irritate us, or do we just grit our teeth and go in? How about shifting gears when we are about to gossip about somebody and pray for him instead? And so on. We shall find that the oftener we pray, the more we shall be driven to prayer.

"Being watchful in it." This means that we be alert and active in our prayer, of course; we dare not come before our gracious King with halfhearted mumblings. But there is more in it than that. This watchfulness is the watchfulness of men who are waiting for their Lord's return; this is the alertness of men who know that they are living in the world's last days and would be ready when the Lord comes suddenly, as come He will.

"With thanksgiving." Luther once said that if prayer is incense that rises up before the throne of God, thanksgiving is a bed of fiery coals in the censer which makes the incense rise with a fine, soaring buoyancy. When we thank our God for all His gifts, our hearts burn within us, and we grow bold and confident in our asking, for we know that we are asking for already given gifts. The God who gave us His Son will withhold no good thing from us.

"Pray for us also." As watchful men awaiting the hour when our Lord returns to crown our lives with His eternal joy, as thankful men whose rising soul surveys all the mercies of our God, we grow large of heart. We cannot in our praying remain shut in upon ourselves. We pray for all men and implore God's blessing on them all. Perhaps we need to be reminded that there is no man so great and strong that he does not need our prayers; Paul, that mighty man of God, asked for the intercessions of the fumbling saints of Colossae. He knew that he remained always a beggar before God and could do the work he had to do only by the grace continually bestowed on him.

"That God may open to us a door for the Word." Paul the prisoner asks nothing for himself; he asks that God's cause be furthered through him, that God's Word be spoken through him, that he may speak the mystery of Christ as he by God's will and for God's glory ought to speak it.

PRAYER. Lord, teach us to pray. Amen.

What Is Wisdom?

Conduct yourselves wisely toward outsiders, making the most of the time. Col. 4:5

"Conduct yourselves *wisely*." What is wisdom? If polltakers were to ask this question across the country, they would get a wide variety of answers; and no doubt a great many men would be hard put to give any answer at all. Our generation does not apparently put a very high value on wisdom. We discuss men's knowledge, their skill, their competence, their eloquence, their courage, their charm — but do we ever talk about their wisdom? Yet wisdom is all-important; Paul calls for wisdom just here, in an area of life that is of supreme importance, in our relationship to others. What does he mean by wisdom? How does one act "wisely toward outsiders"?

We cannot separate wisdom from Christ; Paul, apostle of Jesus Christ by the will of God, has told us that in Christ "are hid all the treasures of *wisdom* and knowledge" (Colossians 2:3). When Paul proclaims Christ, he is "teaching every man in all wisdom" (Colossians 1:28). To conduct oneself wisely is to conduct oneself Christly; it is to let His Word dwell richly in one's heart, to let Him be in our minds and hearts always. Then we can "teach and admonish one another in all wisdom" (Colossians 3:16). He who is our

Wisdom in our dealings with fellow Christians is to be our Wisdom also in our dealings with "outsiders," with non-Christians. He *must* be, for by Him God has reconciled to Himself "all things, whether on earth or in heaven, making peace by the blood of His cross." (Colossians 1:20)

To conduct ourselves wisely toward outsiders is to know that Christ hung on the cross for these "outsiders," that He shed His blood for these "outsiders," that He made peace for these "outsiders"; it is to know that in the intention of Christ there *are* no "outsiders" at all. He died and rose that there might be no outsiders, that all men might return to the Father's house. We are acting wisely toward outsiders when our every word and work is a living witness to that fact. What that means for our conduct at home, on the road, at work, and in our hours of relaxation need not be spelled out for us in detail. If Christ dwells in us by His Word, if He looms large before our eyes in the glory of His cross, if His love that embraced us and all "outsiders" lives in us, then our duty in each case as each case arises will spell itself out for us imperiously and unmistakably.

To know Christ is to know what time it is, what time it really is by God's clock. The wisdom we find in Christ gives us eyes to see that these days are last days, that all days since Christ move in quickened tempo toward the end of days, that it is now or never for the outsiders — and for us. How shall we answer to the Christ, the Lord of all our time, when He returns if He does not find us "making the most of the time" — the time that He has given us to be His walking, living, acting, winning witness?

PRAYER. Give us, O Lord, the wisdom that is hid in Thee that we may wisely do the work Thou hast given us to do, with Thy love, to Thy glory. Amen.

The Art of Witnessing

Let your speech always be gracious, seasoned with salt, so that you may know how you ought to answer everyone. Col. 4:6

It is important to note what Paul is assuming here: he assumes that we shall *have* to answer people. He takes for granted that we shall be so markedly different from the men who do not call Jesus Lord that people will wonder about us and will be moved to ask us about that hidden center of our lives from which there radiates a strength, a calm, a clean and cheerful self-possession which is in mysterious contrast to the harassed and haunted face of the rest of mankind. He is assuming that the peace of Christ, the Word of Christ, and the name of the Lord Jesus have made us remarkable and marked men who "shine as lights in the world, holding fast the Word of life." (Philippians 2:15)

Paul is assuming also *that* we shall answer; what he is concerned about here is *how* we shall answer. We need not grow self-conscious and diffident about our witness just because we are not mighty masters of words: the simplest words of witness coming from a man whose life has already spoken for him and for his Lord will with God's blessing do the work. In fact it is just the people who pride themselves on their skill in witnessing who fail most often in the "how" of witnessing. A man may know that Jesus came to call sinners *to repentance;* he may know that before God the Judge all men must plead guilty if they would find in Him God the Deliverer. He knows this, and he knows how to say it. In mistaken zeal he heavy-handedly and not without some self-righteousness spells out the Law to his inquirer; he becomes the judge of the sinner, perhaps unconsciously, and repels and antagonizes him before the sinner has had a chance to hear the Good News which God wants him to hear. "Let your speech always be *gracious,*" Paul tells us. Jesus compared *His* call to repentance to the calling of a mother bird; our call to repentance should be as winsome and as inwardly compelling as that.

"Let your speech be . . . seasoned with salt," is Paul's second word concerning the manner of our witnessing. One wonders how many men have been repelled by insipid and tasteless words uttered by well-intentioned people. Are we really witnessing to the Jesus whom the apostles proclaimed and the evangelists portrayed when we confront men with sugary sentiments and sentimental verses that make the strong Son of God look like those weak, cheap, pink-and-blue pictures of Him? Is this the Son of Man who drove out demons, bade the sea be still, and was consumed by zeal for His Father's house? Is this the Lion of Judah who for us men and our salvation fought the grim, victorious battle with death?

We cannot answer the inquirer by quoting Bible passages to him, at least not always and usually not at first; the language of the Bible is so strange to him that we shall have to translate it into terms he can understand; we must in this, as in other things, try to do what Paul did: "become all things to all men." We must find men where they live and speak a speech that is living speech *for them.* But if we live with our Bible and learn *its* clean and chaste majestic language, *its* way of recounting the mighty acts of God; if we let this Word of God shape and guide our thought and speech, we shall find that we can witness to the inquirer with a sound and seasoned speech that will not repel him, that will not diminish or obscure the overwhelming gracious majesty of Him whom we call Lord.

PRAYER. O Lord, let Thy Spirit lead us into all truth that we may witness to Thee graciously in seasoned speech. Amen.

Gracious Name-Dropper

Tychicus . . . a beloved brother and . . . fellow servant in the Lord . . . Onesimus, the faithful and beloved brother, who is one of yourselves. . . . Aristarchus, my fellow prisoner . . . Mark, the cousin of Barnabas . . . and Jesus, who is called Justus. . . . They have been a comfort to me. Epaphras . . . a servant of Christ Jesus . . . always remembering you earnestly in his prayers. . . . He has worked hard for you. . . . Luke, the beloved physician. Col. 4:7-14

The name-dropper has a bad reputation, and he deserves it. He drops into conversation the names of important and charming people whom everybody would like to know and makes it pretty plain that *he,* the dropper of names, knows these persons very well indeed. In one operation he feeds his pride and builds up his importance in the eyes of others. A very nasty kind of man.

Paul is a great name-dropper. But with a difference, a diametrical difference. The people Paul mentions could not possibly add to his prestige; in fact, one may safely say of them that if Paul had not mentioned them, no one would ever have heard of them at all. Paul has given them whatever immortality of fame they may possess. He does not characterize them all, but he makes plain that he loves and values them all as his brothers, his fellow servants, faithful, beloved, his fellow prisoners, men who are a comfort to him. A generous, warm light falls on them all.

91

Perhaps Paul had only intelligent and completely lovable people around him. Perhaps he was not beset and irritated by the stupid, bungling, inept, and unlovable people *we* have to deal with, the kind we mention with an easy irony or bury in silence. Perhaps; but it is not likely. We do not know much about them, but what we do know about some of them indicates that they were not altogether lovely and lovable saints.

Paul's First Letter to Timothy makes clear that this beloved child of Paul's was, for all his fine qualities, a timid soul in need of considerable bracing up and inclined to worrying overmuch about his stomach.

Epaphras, whom Paul commends so warmly, was a good and faithful man, instant in prayer and deeply concerned about the church which he had founded at Colossae. But he was in all probability no great light intellectually; he was unable to cope with the false teaching that threatened his church and had to call on Paul for help.

Mark had once been a bitter disappointment to Paul; Paul and Barnabas had taken him along on their missionary journey through Cyprus and into Asia Minor, and Mark ran off for home and mother before the journey was half done. Paul even quarreled with Barnabas over Mark, Barnabas' cousin.

And Onesimus, "the faithful and beloved brother" — that is all Paul says of him; these words are a brief but mighty document of Christian forgiveness. For Onesimus was a slave, a thief, and a runaway; but that is past, that is forgiven, that is buried in the depths of the sea. The Christians of Colossae are not told that or reminded of it (they probably knew it, for Onesimus' master, Philemon, was a member of the church at Colossae).

A man gets this kind of love and becomes this kind of name-dropper when he becomes a servant of Jesus Christ, the great Forgiver of us all. We are all God's thievish runaways; we have all robbed Him and deserted Him. If we are still beloved, it is because we have been forgiven and restored. We can become credible witnesses to God the Father of our Lord Jesus Christ only if we forgive one another and become name-droppers after the manner of Paul, the servant of Jesus Christ.

PRAYER. Give Thy servants, O God, the grace to forgive as they have been forgiven, that all their speech may be a winning witness to Thy love. Amen.

A Blessing from Jail

I, Paul, write this greeting with my own hand. Remember my fetters. Grace be with you. Col. 4:18

As Paul reaches for the pen to write the closing greeting with his own hand (he dictated the body of the letter), he is reminded that his is a fettered hand. And so the apostle's last words to his friends and brothers at Colossae is both a request for their sympathy and prayers ("Remember my fetters") and a blessing upon them ("Grace be with you").

That is the story of the apostle and of the apostolic church in all its human weakness and in all its divine power. The apostle is fettered; the grace of God, which is his to have and to give, is not fettered: it breaks forth from jail and speeds on and triumphs in the apostle's Word. "Grace be with you!" — that sums up once more all that Paul has told the Colossians and given to the Colossians in his letter, all the undeserved and lavish love of God, which delivered them from the dominion of darkness and gave them His Son to be their Lord and King, Christ the Image of God, in whom they behold their Father's face, Christ the Creator and Preserver of the heaven and earth and all the powers therein, Christ the Head of the church, the crucified and risen Reconciler of all men and all things, the Hope of Glory, the One in whom all wisdom and knowledge are hidden, the Liberator from all crawling, superstitious fears, before whom all powers in heaven and on earth must bow. Not least of the blessings given by God in Christ is the gentle yoke of the Christ, the fact that His grace lays hold of our disordered lives and makes our round of duties in this world a service rendered to Him. This grace no fetters can bind; it will go forth, and it does go forth. It comes to us to bless us as we read.

We are all of us bound and fettered in one way or another; we all live and work within limitations. We are fettered by our frail humanity and by the strong sins that still cling to us; we are limited by physical disabilities, by our diffidence and shyness, by our lack of insight into other people's hopes and fears, by our lack of tact in approaching our fellowman, by the insufficiency of our knowledge, by our lack of skill in speech. Some of us are limited by the narrowness of our lives; we may have but small opportunity to mingle with men. None of us is so strong and great in Christ that he is sufficient to himself; even the strongest and greatest needs his fellow Christians' sympathy and their prayers, needs his brothers' word.

But none of us is so little, so weak, so fettered that he cannot be a vessel for the grace of God, that he cannot in some measure reflect upon others the light that has shined on him. God has willed it so; He has willed that "we have this treasure in earthen vessels, to show that the transcendent power belongs to God and not to us." We are all earthen vessels, cheap and fragile ware; but God pours oil into each bowl and lights a wick in it so that even the cheapest and most fragile bowl can be a lamp to light up one corner of the world.

PRAYER. O God of all grace, give us Thy grace, and make us vessels of Thy grace; through Jesus Christ, our Lord. Amen.